Really important stuff

my Kids have taught me

by Cynthia Copeland Lewis

Workman Publishing, New York

Library of Congress Cataloging-in-Publication Data

Lewis, Cynthia Copeland
Really important stuff my kids have taught me/ by Cynthia Copeland Lewis.
p. cm.
ISBN 1-56305-700-X (pbk.)
1. Children—quotations. I. Title.
PN6328.C5L42 1994
305.23—dc20   94-31588
CIP

Workman books are available at special discounts when purchased in bulk for
premiums and sales promotions as well as for fund-raising or educational use.
Special editions or book excerpts can also be created to specification. For details,
contact the Special Sales Director at the address below.

Workman Publishing Company, Inc.
708 Broadway, New York, NY 10003

Manufactured in the United States of America
First printing October 1994

10 9 8 7 6 5 4 3 2

For my mother,
who has taught me almost as much
as my children have.

*D*on't tell my kids this, but they've taught me a lot more than I've taught them. When I listen to my children, I am amazed at the insight and clarity they bring to issues I'm still struggling to understand. My red-cheeked daughter in her wet snowsuit can't define persistence or discuss its value as a character trait. But she's figured out that if she wants in, she'll just have to keep banging until someone opens the door. Her younger sister has not studied the art of presentation and persuasion, but she knows that wearing pajamas with feet may not help her win an argument for a later bedtime.

And my son often reminds me that a little kiss can make a big difference.

If you are fortunate enough to have your own children, continue to appreciate their wisdom. If not, put away your newspaper the next time you are sitting on a park bench and tune in to the conversation in the sandbox. You might learn something.

I've gathered within the following pages an assortment of smart, funny, innocent, perfectly sensible things my kids have taught me over the years. Read on and remind yourself how simple everything really is.

Jump right in or you might change your mind about swimming.

Speak up.

It's more fun to color outside the lines.

If you're going to
draw on the wall,
do it behind the couch.

You can make chores fun by telling everyone you're Cinderella.

If the flowers you draw don't look like anyone elses, that's good.

It's possible to feel full
when it comes to
more vegetables, but not
full when it comes
to a piece of cake.

Hang on tight.

Sometimes it's
smart to be scared.

If you're going to bother wetting the soap and messing up the towel, you might just as well go ahead and wash your hands.

Pants with
pockets
are better.

Ask why until
you understand.

Always have something in your lunchbox that you can trade with.

Don't say you brushed your teeth if you really didn't.

You can be anything
you want to be
when you grow up.

Take it apart
to see how
it works.

Even if you've been
fishing for three hours
and haven't gotten
anything except poison
ivy and a sunburn,
you're still better
off than the worm.

Look at it upside down.

Don't expect
a stranger
to wipe
your nose.

If you want pancakes for breakfast, offer to help make them.

Some weeks you
really need Saturday
on a Wednesday.

Don't giggle until
after you've swallowed
your milk.

You can either
keep pedaling, get
off the bike, or
fall over.

Shortcuts aren't always.

Thinking about getting a shot is a lot worse than getting one.

Explore.

You don't find
snakes—
they find you.

Wander.

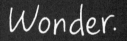

Even if you make a really nice place for it to live, with grass and dirt and a few rocks and sticks, the caterpillar will still spend all its time trying to get out of the jar.

Play, don't watch.

You think your book bag is the heaviest until you pick up someone else's by mistake.

On the playground
you're either chasing
or being chased.

Sometimes two
is a crowd.

You can't stop the sled halfway down the hill.

Hitting the kid with the ball might get you the ball, but it won't get you anyone to throw it to.

Give yourself a nickname before someone else does.

Don't tease a big kid.

Lick your ice-cream cone before it gets a chance to melt.

Getting up early gives you more time to play.

Hot lunch
sounds better
than it tastes.

Go barefoot.

Grandmothers don't mind
hearing the same story
over and over,
but other people do.

When you're the one
setting the table,
you can give the
funny fork
to your sister.

All people look silly
when they yawn.

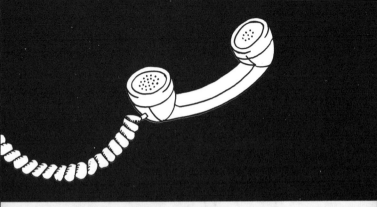

If you answer the phone, be sure you're ready to remember the message.

Puppies are cute,
but they
have sharp teeth.

Whiners usually

Watching ants is fun.

Who cares what happened last week?

You always spill juice
when you're wearing your
Sunday School clothes.

Every time you swim
out to the rock,
it gets a little closer.

Trust people.

WELCOME

The key is
usually under
the mat.

It doesn't count if your swing is going the highest if you're getting pushed.

Knock first.

Look at the
footprints
you've made.

Bees shouldn't be
so nice and fuzzy.

Don't worry about crossing the street until you get to the curb.

Cheer!

Make sure you always know where the bathroom is.

When you hear a noise in the closet, it's scarier not to open the door and peek in.

Insist on doing it yourself.

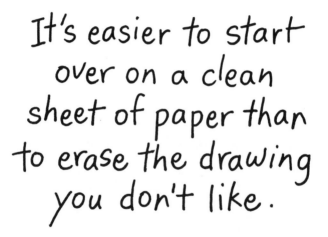

It's easier to start over on a clean sheet of paper than to erase the drawing you don't like.

Hiding peas
under your napkin
only works once.

No one should
wear white pants.

If you are going
to lose a mitten,
you might as well
lose the pair.

Plain underwear
is boring.

On the first day of school, sit in the middle of the bus.

More is not
always better.

Look both ways.

Before you climb the tree, make sure your mother is close enough to hear you holler if you need help on the way down.

Don't nod
on the phone.

If you toss the ball to another kid, he'll probably toss it back.

Be nice to the lunch lady.

You only go down the slide headfirst one time.

If you wait until you're really sure, you'll never take off the training wheels.

Giggle.

Make up the rules
as you go along.

Recycle.

If you try to catch two butterflies with one net, they'll both get away.

Don't blow bubbles
into the wind.

Leave a light on in
case you have to go
to the bathroom
in the night.

Three hops get
you just as far
as one leap.

It's easier to spend
the money in your
grandfather's pocket than
the money in your own.

It's okay to order vanilla even if rainbow bubble gum ice cream is on the menu.

Flowers and pricker bushes grow out of the same dirt.

Make waves.

If you don't like
the birthday girl,
don't go to the party.

Enjoy the ride.

Look behind
the puppet theater.

Don't say "The last one there is a rotten egg" unless you're absolutely sure there's a slow kid behind you.

Scribble.

Don't expect your friends to be as excited about your "100" as you are.

It does matter
who started it.

Yell if you want
to be heard.

Skipping is
hard to do.

If you have bunk beds, you might as well sleep on top.

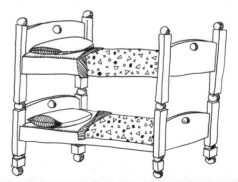

Stamp your feet
when you get angry.

People know
when you're letting
them win.

Ask for sprinkles.

Lunch tastes better out of a Power Ranger lunch box than out of a brown paper bag.

Open your
eyes
under water.

Don't try diving for the
first time in front of
a bunch of people.

Use the
fancy soap.

Trade fair.

Remember everyone's favorite color.

When you're being dragged, let go of the leash.

You're tall enough
when you can reach
the light switch.

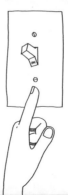

One hundred
is a lot.

If your mother wants
to hold your hand,
there's probably
a good reason.

Frogs do not
look alike.

You'll have a lot more
respect for a
bird after you try
making a nest.

Anything can
be a toy.

Kids aren't supposed
to have
clean fingernails.

Apologize for it before
your mother notices
the stain on your shirt.

You have to love your brother, even if he doesn't deserve it.

Don't forget to say your prayers.

Try the grown-up rake before you decide to use the kid rake.

Let Santa surprise you.

"Follow the Leader"
is a lot more fun
if you're the leader.

Nobody likes a tattletale.

The harder the wind blows, the higher your kite will fly.

Big dogs have
big appetites.

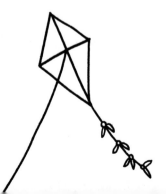

Using a word you don't understand can be embarrassing.

If you're going
to laugh,
laugh out loud.

Know just when
to jump
off the swing.

Don't save
time – use it up.

Even babies like
to grab for
things just beyond
their reach.

Know what you like.

Climbing the hill is more fun than standing on top.

One thing you
can't pretend to be
is funny.

Homesick is
the worse kind
of sick.

If you want to see a shooting star, you might have to spend a lot of nights looking up.

Don't always
act your age.

If splashing in puddles means you have to wear wet shoes for the rest of the day, sometimes it's worth it.

The end isn't
always where
it should be.

Don't wear it
if it itches.

It's easier to knock
on a door that's
not shut all the way.

If the horse you're
drawing looks more
like a dog,
make it a dog.

Never start
slowly.

You're only little
until someone littler
comes along.

Make up a reason to have a party.

It's not really giving
if you give away the
animal crackers with
missing heads and feet.

Save a place in line
for your friends.

Help
yourself.

Remember who gives wet kisses, and the next time you see them, wave from across the room.

Be the first one
to make footprints
in new snow.

Nobody can pedal the bike for you.

If it smells bad, it will taste that way too.

People will notice
your feet
if you wear
two different socks.

Just because you can't
spell doesn't mean
you can't write
a good story.

Don't laugh
if you don't
get the joke.

The teacher can always
tell when you did
your homework
on the bus.

Practice until
you can whistle.

Nobody notices it when
your zipper is up, but
everyone notices
when it's down.

Be early
if you're a bird,
and late
if you're a worm.

Always try at least one bite.

Sometimes you have to take the test before you've finished studying.

Recess is
the best part.

Math is fun when you're counting jellybeans.

Half a nap
is worse
than none.

It's easier to do work for a teacher you like.

Wear party
shoes to parties.

Don't squeeze
your gerbil.

If you're going
to fight,
use pillows.

Demand your turn
in the front seat.

The colder you look when you come inside, the bigger the cup of hot chocolate you'll get.

Believe in
Santa Claus.

Don't wet your pants in school more than once.

Stick up for your brother.

If it doesn't bleed,
you won't
get much sympathy.

Don't blow out
somebody elses
birthday candles.

If you have to drop it,
drop it jelly-side up.

It feels a lot colder
when you're shoveling snow
than when you're building
a snow fort.

Before you trade
sandwiches, check
between the bread.

Where you're going
is more important
than where you stand.

Big clothes make
you feel smaller.

Don't argue for a later bedtime while you're wearing pajamas with feet.

It's hard not to
pick at it.

Don't dump a puzzle
on the floor unless
you have the time
to put it together.

Have a hanky
tucked up
your sleeve.

Ten minutes is short
if it's a recess and long
if it's a punishment.

The same bump feels a
lot different to the person
in the front of the
bus than it does to
the person in the back.

A little kiss
can make a
big difference.

Being captain doesn't mean you're the smartest one, it just means you're the one with the boat.

You have to eat
a lot of cereal
before you find
the free toy.

If your feet
don't reach the ground,
let them swing.

Once you're wet
it doesn't matter
how much more
you get rained on.

When you bring a salamander to school, you find you have lots of friends you didn't even know about.

Getting lost teaches
you how to read a map.

Silence can be
an answer.

Be afraid of a
kid who is
never afraid.

**Ask where
things come
from.**

You can't unspill a
spilled glass of milk.

Just keep going.

If you want a kitten, start out asking for a horse.

Little crayons still make bright marks.

You won't catch
a whale with a worm.

Picking your nose
when no one is
looking is still
picking your nose.

If you can't name it,
scrape it
off your pizza.

If you want someone
to listen to what
you're saying, whisper it.

It's hard not to like someone who likes you.

Don't answer until
you're ready to.

Hug people for
no reason.

If you don't
get it, say so.

Everybody loves
a backrub.

Never, ever, miss the
fireworks on the
the Fourth of July.

Fresh air is
good for you.

If it tastes good,
it probably isn't
good for you.

Write your name
everywhere.

Just keep banging
until someone
opens the door.

Don't mix up
your b's and d's.

Making your bed is a waste of time.

Wave to people
you don't know.

There is no good
reason why clothes
have to match.

Hang your best picture on the refrigerator.

Milk tastes a lot better through a straw.

Everyone's afraid of funny noises at night.

Take turns.

Whether you're in or out, you usually want to be the other.

If a lady
has a black
thing on her tooth,
tell her.

A band-aid
always makes
it feel better.

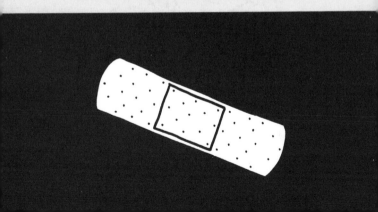

The fuzzier, the better.

Why buy roses when daisies are free?

If you start out
afraid of the dark,
pretty soon you'll be
afraid of the dusk
too.

You feel a lot braver
the second time you
jump out of the tree.

Don't sit down
until the game
is over.

If you can't find
a way through the
crowd, make one.

If it's going to be
two against one,
make sure
you're not the one.

Wishing you knew
how to jump
rope isn't enough.

Sharing isn't always
the right thing —
like when it's
chicken pox.

Don't wait for
someone to ask
if you're hungry.

Crying gets you
more attention,
but not more friends.

Smile at the
bus driver.

When it's your shovel,
you're in charge
of the sand castle.

It's a lot harder
to laugh when
you're by yourself.

Babies get
more
attention.

Seashells should always be found, not bought.

Wait for your
little sister.

Before you logroll
down the hill,
check for rocks.

You might never get called on if you don't raise your hand.

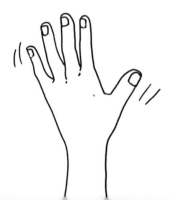

When in doubt,
order a hot dog.

Squeeze the tube slowly, because once the toothpaste is out, it's pretty hard to get it back in.

It can't hurt
to ask for
a fourth wish.

They'll remember you if
you're the best reader in
class – or if you
throw up at lunch.

When you've just caught the football, the tackle doesn't hurt as much.

Just do
your best.

Nobody will lend you
an umbrella
when it's raining.

Even Popeye didn't eat
his spinach until
he absolutely had to.

Usually you learn
your lesson, but
you don't always
remember it.

As soon as you
can walk, you
never want
to crawl again.

**Let the frog go
where you
found it.**

Sometimes the squeaky wheel gets kicked.

If it hurts, stop doing it.

It's hard to like
the piano if you
are forced to
take lessons.

To make a see-saw work, you have to take turns being down.

Giving away one cookie when you only have two is harder than giving away ten when you have a whole batch.

If you want to make
a friend at the beach
start building a
really big sand castle.

The school bus is
never running late
the same day
you are.

Dads don't yell as
much as Moms,
but they yell louder.

Big fish
eat
little fish.

If your dog doesn't like someone, you probably shouldn't either.

How do you know you
can't make a rocket
out of tin foil boxes
and cardboard
unless you try?

Poems don't have
to rhyme.

If you don't run, you
won't trip, but
you may never get there.

Children's tea parties are more fun than grown-ups' tea parties.

Sometimes it's the littlest kid who fights hardest.

No one does much living in the living room.

Believing in the Tooth Fairy is easier than trying to figure out how else the money gets under your pillow.

Don't jump out
of the apple
tree with cardboard
wings.

Toads aren't ugly —
they're just toads.

You can teach an old dog new tricks with the right kind of doggie treats.

It's more fun to
ask questions
than to answer them.

A kid who can't skate
says he has lousy skates.

There are names that hurt much more than sticks and stones.

Don't dive deeper
than you have
breath for.

Don't pop someone else's bubble.

If it's in your way,
climb over it.

No matter what the teacher says, February is the longest month.

Be polite.

Mean dogs have
mean owners.

Aim before you blow
your straw paper.

A penny saved
is not much.

Your echo
will always
answer.

If you're going to take just one step, make it a giant step.

Rest your head
on the nearest lap.

Sometimes you need
a little push to go down
the big slide.

Say grace.

If you stay clean
you'll never have fun.

Wish on
the
first star.

Eat chocolate chip cookies when they're still warm.

Get in line
when
the bell rings.

Imaginary friends
can be the best.

Count the money
in your piggy bank
once a week.

All libraries
smell the same.

It's more fun to clean a new bike than an old one.

If somebody calls
you a crybaby,
don't cry.

If you want to get carried, pretend to fall asleep in the back seat of the car.

You don't have to
own the swing
to enjoy it.

Don't let the spaghetti
sauce leak
onto your greenbeans.

Put your name
on your scissors.

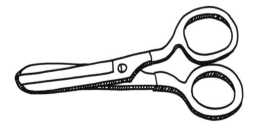

You won't get out of doing the dishes by breaking a cup — you'll just end up vacuuming the floor, too.

One hundred times
is not too
many when it's your
favorite book.

If someone does'nt understand what you're saying, keep repeating it until he does.

Dirt is only considered bad when it's not on the ground.

A pencil without an eraser might just as well be a pen.

Stop when
you're full.

No one likes
to be left
alone.

The longer the test,
the better you feel
when it's over.

Don't be a copycat.

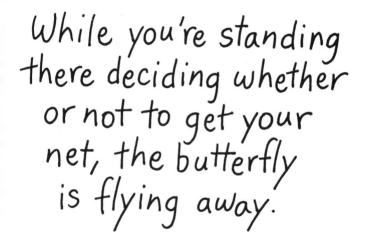
While you're standing there deciding whether or not to get your net, the butterfly is flying away.

Every day
comes with
a day after.

If you want to zoom down the expert slope tomorrow, you have to fall down the bunny slope today.

You work so hard
pedaling up the hill
that you hate to brake
on the way down.

Get up before
the dew is gone.

Sometimes you find the neatest dragonfly when you're out looking for tadpoles.

Take the day as it comes.

Every good has
a better and every
bad a worse.

You won't taste
the medicine
when it's stirred
into your juice.

The fastest kid in the class shouldn't get a head start.

Sometimes you complain about hot lunch just because you're used to complaining about hot lunch.

Don't take eight
doughnuts if
your stomach only
holds two.

You can think
better in front of
a clear blackboard.

Stretch.

Slugs leave an easy trail
to follow, but
who really wants to?

Being generous is giving away half your sandwich when it's peanut butter and jelly, not when it's liverwurst.

You have to be
ready to jump when
the rope swings
under your feet.

A tiny hole
can empty a great
big bucket.

Every piece of the puzzle that doesn't fit gets you closer to finding the one that does.

If the flowers wilt, water them.

A snow day is more fun than a vacation day.

Ask if you
can play, too.

If you can't swim, wade.

If a kid isn't paying attention, maybe it's because the person talking isn't saying anything worth listening to.

You don't get to decide your part in the school play, but you do get to decide whether or not you play it well.

There isn't a lot of time between green bananas and speckled bananas.

Half the fun of pizza is sharing it.

It's not enough to be able to spell "magnificence" in your bedroom, you have to be able to spell it at the microphone during the spelling bee.

Sometimes the
biggest apple
has the
biggest worm.

It's hard to
measure
a crooked line.

You can't be
everyone's
best friend.

Stay close enough to the campfire to keep warm, but not so close that you get scorched.

Sometimes when you're first, you get stuck holding the door open for everyone else.

When you're lost,
it's better to stand
still than to follow
the wrong path.

Learning how is
more important
than learning what.

If you can't reach
someone, blow kisses.

There's always
a fancier
skateboard.

Old shoes
are more
comfortable.

It's easier to climb
a tree that leans.

Ride the waves
to shore.

In every line, someone has to be first and someone has to be last.

Celery with peanut butter and raisins tastes better if you call it "ants on a log".

If someone else
has done it,
you can too.

Listen to the
teacher.

One drop of black paint
from your brush clouds
the whole cup of water.

Sometimes it's hard
to tell if you're
leading the group
or being pushed.

If you want to make
friends with a bird,
you can't run at it.

In checkers you have to think ahead or else you're going to get jumped.

If there aren't any shadows, there isn't enough light.

Forgive your fishing
buddy fast, so you
can get back to
digging worms together.

You run faster than you thought you could when you're being chased by a bumblebee.

It's easier to throw sticks on the campfire than to try to restart it when it goes out.

Just because you're
wearing cowboy boots
doesn't mean you can
ride a horse.

Sometimes you clap just because everyone around you is.

The kid who cries
the hardest isn't always
the one with the
biggest boo-boo.

If the tree had apples last year, don't expect pears this year.

Collect things.

You'll have to eat a little dirt along the way.

Everything looks
different
through tears.

A little sugar
can go
a long way.

It doesn't matter how fast you're running with the football if you're going in the wrong direction.

Every castle has
a dungeon.

Build the base of your block tower wider than the top.

Be sure.

Sometimes tomorrow takes a really long time to come.

It's hard to sleep on a strange pillow.

When you're dressed up like a princess, it's easier to act like one.

Don't blow on a spark unless you want a fire.

Sometimes you have to scream on the way down.

Invite yourself over.

Don't be too
curious
about hornets.

It's easier to see
the mistakes
on someone else's
paper.

Leave something behind.

When you're told not to put raisins up your nose, it's hard to think about anything else.

If you play tag with the big kids, be prepared to be "it" for a while.

The path you're on
looks different
when you turn around.

Wait your turn.

You can make your crystal ball say whatever you want it to.

Sometimes the best one in the play has the fewest lines.

Jump at the chance.

Wearing a halo can give you a headache after a while.

It's hard to unlearn a bad word.

You're more likely to get lost in the dark.

If you stand on tiptoe to be measured this year, you'll have to stand on tiptoe for the rest of your life.

Do what you can.

If you keep pretending
you know how to
swim, one day someone's
going to push you
in the pool for fun
– but it won't be.

Don't run away
from home in the
middle of a storm.

The first sip
is the best.

Every blizzard starts out with a few flakes.

You don't see the dimples without the smile.

Sometimes the biggest fights are over the smallest things.

It's hard to know
how far a branch
will bend before
it breaks.

Crawling
still gets
you there.

Carry your own flashlight when you walk down a dark path.

Keep your eye on the ball.

Chasing the cat is more fun than catching it.

It's not how many
dolls you have —
it's how much fun
you have playing with
them that matters.

Your room
gets smaller
as you get
bigger.

The longer the rain storm, the happier you are to see the sun.

Check
under
the
bed.

If you keep missing,
get closer to the basket.

A ten dollar bill
doesn't do much good
if the candy machine
only takes quarters.

Anybody can skate on smooth ice.

Fill in the blanks.

Sometimes the medicine is worse than the cough.

As soon as you understand two times four, you can't believe there was a time when you didn't understand it.

Watch where you're going.

Don't wait to be discovered.

Even Superman probably tries to fly higher and faster.

It doesn't take long to pick up the toys when everybody helps.

The harder you throw a ball at the ground, the higher it bounces.

You can't change your mind once the egg is scrambled.

Every drop
of rain
adds to
the ocean.

If you don't want your house to be haunted, stop believing in ghosts.

Wait for the curtain to come down before you start to clap.

You can't ask
to start over
just because you're
losing the game.

It's easier
to be cheerful
on a full
stomach.

Get up if you fall down.

Some nights it's not worth fighting over who gets the top bunk.

Don't be so afraid
of losing your Frisbee
that you never
throw it.

Even summer
has mosquitoes
and sunburn.

Make your mother proud of you.

Your shadow
will do exactly
what you want
it to do.

Once your mother finds your broken glasses, you can't keep saying they're not broken.

Remember to say thank you.

You can sit around and wait for a ride, or you can start walking.

There are always a
few unpopped kernels
at the bottom of
the popcorn bucket.

If you want to find
a new hideout in
the woods, you'll have
to leave the trail.

Learn it by heart.

You need to give the guy a ticket before you get on the ride.

Making a cake is mostly about licking the bowl.

The fewer promises you make, the more you keep.

Sometimes your best move is blocked by your own checkers.

Turn over rocks
to see what's
under them.

Don't drop
the ball.

There are a lot
of different ways
to get to the top
of the jungle gym.

Try not
to forget
your dreams.

The bad guy
doesn't always
wear a black hat.

Red, white, and blue
always go together.

As soon as you tell
a secret, it's not one.

Make peace.

Food tastes
better at a picnic.

As long as you don't look ahead in the workbook, you can make it through today's lesson.

Sometimes saving for a rainy day means you don't have as much fun when it's sunny.

You can try on
your fathers shoes,
but you can't walk
very well in them.

If you're going
to pull it up,
pull it up
by the roots.

Pick up your
little sister
when she falls
down.

You'll never catch
a frog if you're
worried about getting
your shorts wet.

Every time you pass him, pat the dog.

Every flower
smells a little
different.

Pack your raincoat
in your book bag, but
don't take it out until
you feel a few drops.

You can't always be first.

You will learn a lot
about your neighbors
when you set up
a lemonade stand
on the sidewalk.

It's only fun to play
school when you get
to be the teacher.

You won't get to
see the Big Dipper
if you're afraid
of the dark.

Twelve is a lot older than eight.

Go to the bathroom before you get into the car.

It's hard to save
the best for last.